WELCOME TO THE BISHOP'S PALACE AND EARL'S PALACE, KIRKWALL

For centuries Kirkwall was the capital of the Norse earldom of the *Nordreyjar* (the Northern Isles). That ended in 1469 when Christian I of Norway failed to pay the dowry promised to his son-in-law, James III of Scotland, and the latter called in the debt by assuming sovereignty of the Northern Isles. Kirkwall still retains many signs of its former political and ecclesiastical importance – the narrow winding streets, the burghal mansion of Tankerness House (now the Orkney Museum), mighty St Magnus Cathedral and, in its shadow, the picturesque ruins of the 12th-century Bishop's Palace and the Earl's Palace, built around 1600. These two palaces are among the most fascinating medieval buildings in all of Scotland.

Above: The seal impression of Bishop Robert Reid, who undertook a major rebuilding of the Bishop's Palace in the 1550s.

CONTENTS

Left: Bishop Reid's Tower, known locally as the Moosie Too'er, at the north end of the Bishop's Palace. The Earl's Palace lies beyond.

THE BISHOP'S PALACE AND EARL'S PALACE AT A GLANCE

The Bishop's Palace, one of the oldest surviving fortified residences in Scotland, was built in the mid-12th century, at around the same time as St Magnus Cathedral, to provide the bishop with a suitably grand residence. It was here in 1263 that King Hakon IV of Norway died following his disastrous encounter with Alexander III of Scotland at the battle of Largs. Around 1600, Patrick Stewart, the notoriously cruel earl of Orkney, incorporated what was then left of the ancient palace into his extravagant and extraordinary new residence, the Earl's Palace. His creation has justly been hailed as 'possibly the most mature and accomplished piece of Renaissance architecture left in Scotland'.

Opposite: Bishop Reid's Tower stands in the foreground of this 1821 painting by William Daniel, with the Earl's Palace behind.

FAMOUS AND INFAMOUS

14 BISHOP ROBERT REID
Bishop Reid (1541–58), credited as the founder of Edinburgh University, extensively reconstructed the Bishop's Palace.

24 EARL PATRICK STEWART
Earl Patrick (d. 1615) used forced labour to build the Earl's Palace, as well as other castles on Orkney and Shetland.

26 MARQUIS OF MONTROSE
The marquis, the leader of the Royalist forces, briefly occupied the Earl's Palace in 1650.

GRAND EXTERIORS

6 BISHOP REID'S TOWER
With parapets (right) and gun holes, the Bishop's Tower was amply equipped for firearm defence.

16 FRONTISPIECE
Above the elaborate doorway into the Earl's Palace are the arms of Earl Patrick and the royal arms of Scotland.

18 ORIEL WINDOWS
With their corbelled bases, the remains of these windows on the Earl's and Bishop's palaces are unsurpassed in Scotland.

THE NORSE CONNECTION

11 EARL ROGNVALD

The Norse ruler of Orkney, who commissioned the building of St Magnus Cathedral, was the crusading companion of Kirkwall's first bishop.

12 KING HAKON IV
Hakon IV, the last king of Norway to rule over Argyll and the Hebrides, died in the Bishop's Palace on 15 December 1263.

13 SCANDINAVIAN COMB
This fine Scandinavian-type comb testifies to the connection between Kirkwall and Norway.

NOOKS AND CRANNIES

23 FIREPLACE

This magnificent fireplace in the great hall of the Earl's Palace boasts a coronet and the earl's initials on its columns.

6 GUN HOLE

This twinned gun hole on Bishop Reid's Tower was probably altered by Earl Patrick.

22 ANTE-ROOM
This beautifully vaulted little chamber may have been a waiting room for those seeking an audience with Earl Patrick.

A TOUR OF THE BISHOP'S PALACE

The Bishop's Palace as we see it today is all that remains of a much more extensive episcopal residence. This comprised a chapel and two large square towers, one of them – the Manse Tower – of such great size that it possibly housed the bishop's private quarters. The building we know as the Bishop's Palace probably began life as the bishop's great hall.

Bishop Reid's Tower
This 16th-century addition to the Bishop's Palace served as the bishop's private apartment.

Interior
Only the ground floor of this once two-storied building survives.

Corbelling
There are circular window bases like this on both sides of the Bishop's Palace.

East front
This round arch was once the main gate into the episcopal precinct.

The Earl's Palace
For a tour of the Earl's Palace, turn to page 16.

THE EXTERIOR

The formidable bulk of Bishop Reid's Tower dominates Palace Road. Pierced at all levels by gun holes, it is crowned by a defensive parapet carried forward on two rows of corbels. Two sculptures stand beside each other at second-floor level. The right-hand one has an armorial shield, which, though now illegible, probably displayed Bishop Reid's coat-of-arms. The other sculpture cannot be Bishop Reid, as it is plainly much older. It may represent Earl Rognvald and date from around 1300. (The present statue is a copy; the original is on display in the Orkney Museum.)

A long stretch of the east front of the palace, in Watergate, has been rebuilt and contains a large round-arched opening, now blocked. This was the main gate opening into the episcopal precinct from Palace Road. It was rebuilt here when Watergate was widened in 1877. Towards the south end of the east front is an arcade of two round arches (now built up), and above them the projecting base of a large oriel window, with corbelling similar to the windows in the Earl's Palace. This was built by Earl Patrick Stewart around 1600, when he incorporated the ancient Bishop's Palace into his new residence.

The west (far) side of the palace still retains evidence of its 12th-century origins – in the alternating red and yellow stonework forming one of the latrines. The three enormous buttresses were built in Bishop Reid's time to counter the thrust from the internal stone vault. Another oriel from Earl Patrick's time survives near the south end.

Above: The sculpture on Bishop Reid's Tower, possibly of the Norse Earl Rognvald, depicts a figure holding what may be a lyre, resting on a footstool.

Above: These mighty buttresses, added in the 16th century, prevented the much older west wall from sagging.

Opposite: The east front of the Bishop's Palace, looking towards St Magnus Cathedral. The road, constructed in the 19th century, previously formed part of the palace courtyard.

Above: The interior of the Bishop's Palace.

THE INTERIOR

The Bishop's Palace was originally constructed in the 12th century as a two-storey building. The first floor housed the great hall, where the bishop presided over lavish feasting and entertainments. The hall also served as the bishop's courtroom. Little survives of the Bishop's Palace today, but clearly visible are the long dark flagstones forming its walls, and the alternating red and yellow stonework forming the internal openings of the eight narrow loopholes through the west wall. These features are identical to the oldest masonry in St Magnus Cathedral.

Above: An entranceway to St Magnus Cathedral. The same alternating red and yellow stonework can be seen in the west wall of the Bishop's Palace.

REMODELLING THE PALACE

Bishop Reid's major remodelling of the palace in around 1550 greatly altered the interior layout. A stone vault was constructed over the ground floor, creating cellars at ground level, a new hall on the first floor and a suite of rooms (probably guest lodgings) above. The large hall had two fireplaces – one in the north wall for those seated at the high table, the other midway along the east wall.

The five-storey Bishop Reid's Tower served as his private apartment. The vaulted basement was a cellar, lit by three gun holes. The first floor, his private hall reserved for more intimate entertaining, was well lit and furnished with a fireplace, wall-cupboards and a latrine. The spiral stair in the south angle led up to his private suite of three rooms, including his bedchamber. The wall-walk at the top was originally covered by a lean-to roof – an acknowledgement of Orkney's blustery winds!

Earl Patrick Stewart made alterations when he incorporated the Bishop's Palace into his own new Earl's Palace in about 1600. The main need was to provide quarters for his 50-strong bodyguard. Bishop Reid's stone vault was removed, and the hall floor lowered by a metre. Two new fireplaces were inserted, though the north fireplace in the hall seems not to have been affected. The floor over the hall was also rearranged, though the detail is sketchy given the paucity of the remains. Bishop Reid's Tower was little altered.

Above: The seal impression of Bishop Robert Reid, on display in the Orkney Museum.

Below: The great hall as it may have looked in the mid-16th century.

THE STORY OF THE
BISHOP'S PALACE

The first cathedral of the Northern Isles was founded at Birsay soon after 1050 by Earl Thorfinn, the most powerful of all the Norse rulers of Orkney. It was there that the body of the murdered Earl Magnus, soon to be acclaimed as a martyr, was laid in 1117, and where miracles were wrought at his tomb. When in 1135 his nephew, Earl Rognvald, set out from Norway to recover his uncle's patrimony, he vowed that, if successful, he would build a stone minster at Kirkwall 'more magnificent than any other in these lands', that he would dedicate it to Earl Magnus the Holy, and that he would transfer the saint's relics and the episcopal see there also.

The building of St Magnus Cathedral began in 1137. By then, Kirkwall had developed into quite a town, with a jarl's (Norse earl's) residence, a church and merchants' booths grouped around the waterfronts. The resiting of the bishop's *cathedra*, or seat, at Kirkwall resulted in the bishop's residence being transferred there too. The bishop at the time was William 'the Old' (1102-68), friend and crusading companion of Earl Rognvald. He was the driving force behind the building of the splendid new cathedral, and, we must assume, the Bishop's Palace also.

Opposite: A 1920s stained glass window in the north transept of St Magnus Cathedral, depicting Earl Rognvald and the cathedral he founded, resting in his right arm.

TIMELINE

c.1102

WILLIAM THE OLD
William, described on this lead plate as 'first bishop', becomes bishop of Orkney.

c.1117

EARL MAGNUS
Magnus, earl of Orkney, is murdered on the orders of his cousin Hakon. Miracle cures are reported at his shrine.

Above: A depiction of how the first Bishop's Palace, known as the Palace of the Yards, might have looked when King Hakon IV and his court arrived in 1263.

ROYAL DEATHS

Late in 1263, the ageing Norwegian king Hakon IV, attempting to return home to Norway following his near-defeat by the Scots at Largs, on the Firth of Clyde, reached Kirkwall with the battered remnants of his proud fleet. The frail monarch took up residence in the Bishop's Palace. Within days he was dead. *Hakon Hakonson's Saga* recounts how the king died in a chamber adjoining the hall. The bishop's chapel, a building separate from the hall, is also mentioned.

'When he arrived at Kirkwall [the saga recounts], he was confined to his bed by his disorder. Having lain for some nights, the illness abated, and he was on foot for three days. On the first day, he walked about in his apartments; on the second, he attended at the bishop's chapel to hear mass; and on the third he went to St Magnus' church, and walked around the shrine of St Magnus.

'…On the Saturday after, the king's disorder increased to such a degree that he lost the use of his speech; and at midnight Almighty God called King Hakon out of his mortal life. On Sunday the royal corpse was carried into the upper hall and laid on a bier. The body was clothed in a rich garb, with a garland on the head, and dressed out as became a crowned monarch. The masters of the lights stood with tapers in their hands, and the whole hall was illuminated.'

THE MAID OF NORWAY

It is likely that the Bishop's Palace was also where the body of Margaret, the seven-year-old granddaughter of Alexander III of Scotland, was placed in September 1290. Margaret, known as the Maid of Norway, died whilst on her way from Norway to be crowned Queen of Scots. Her death left Scotland without an obvious heir to the throne.

Above: This Scandinavian-type comb, dated to between the late 12th and 14th centuries, may have been made in Trondheim, Norway, under whose episcopal jurisdiction Kirkwall came in 1154. The comb was discovered in a trench in what would have been the Bishop's Palace courtyard.

1263

1290

DEATH OF HAKON
Hakon IV of Norway dies in the Bishop's Palace after disaster for the Norse at the battle of Largs.

DEATH OF MARGARET
The body of Margaret, the first Queen Regnant of Scots, is taken to the Bishop's Palace.

THE PALACE IN THE LATER MIDDLE AGES

For much of the Middle Ages, the Bishop's Palace was 'for the most part in ruins', due to neglect and the diverting of the diocesan revenues elsewhere. Then in 1541 Robert Reid, abbot of Kinloss and credited as the founder of Edinburgh University, became bishop of Orkney. Between then and his death in 1558, allegedly from poisoning, Bishop Reid rebuilt the ancient palace, including the great round tower that bears his name.

In 1568, following the Protestant Reformation, the bishop's lands, including the palace, came into the possession of Earl Robert Stewart, Mary Queen of Scot's half brother. His son, the tyrannous Earl Patrick, 'Black Patie', incorporated it into his own new Earl's Palace as part of his ambitious scheme for a fortified and garrisoned enclosure castle (see page 17). But in 1607 Earl Patrick, 'drowned in debt', was forced to hand the complex over to Bishop James Law. During the subsequent rebellion of 1614, Patrick's natural son, Robert, seized both buildings, as well as Kirkwall Castle and St Magnus Cathedral. What happened next is unknown, but the ancient Bishop's Palace was left to fall into decay.

Opposite: The east front of the Bishop's Palace, drawn by Robert Billings in about 1848. The palace has passed from splendour to ruin and back again several times in its long history.

1540

ROYAL VISIT
During his circumnavigation of Scotland, James V lands at Kirkwall and places garrisons in Kirkwall Castle and the Bishop's Palace.

1568

NEW OWNER
The Bishop's Palace and surrounding lands come into the possession of James V's illegitimate son Robert Stewart.

A TOUR OF THE EARL'S PALACE

Earl Patrick's palace comprised an entirely new building of two ranges, linked to the redesigned Bishop's Palace to its west. The area in front, between the two palaces and the cathedral, was made into a spacious forecourt, in which no doubt Earl Patrick mustered the 50 musketeers who always attended him – even when he went to the cathedral to pray!

As it survives today, the Earl's Palace consists of two long ranges set at right angles to each other and fronting north and west respectively. The earl's design for a single enclosure castle was never realised, however. Stumps of side walls at one end of the south wing demonstrate that this range was intended to continue westwards to connect with the Bishop's Palace.

Opposite: The earl's private chambers in the north-west tower, projecting from the main front, as seen from the palace's principal guest chamber in the south wing.

Below: Plans of the ground and first floors of the Earl's Palace. The numbers correspond to the main stair (1), the kitchen fireplace (2), the steward's room (3) and the ante-room (4).

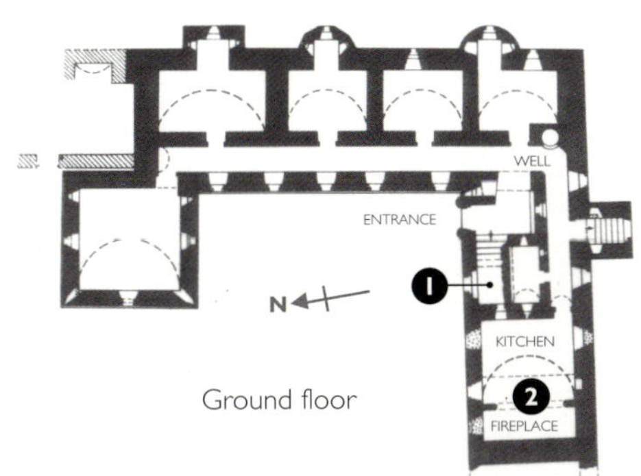

Ground floor

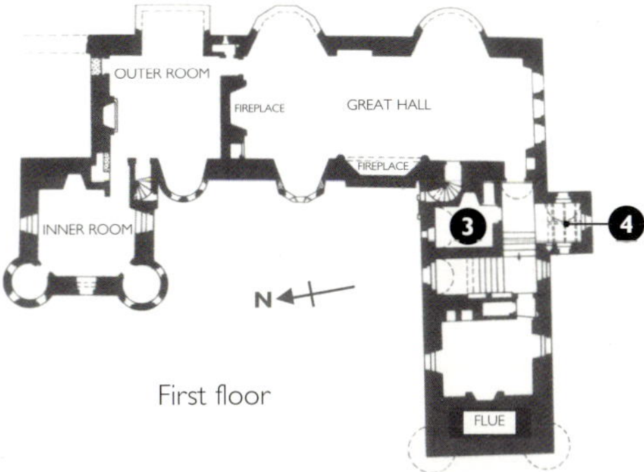

First floor

THE MAIN FRONT

The Earl's Palace is a building of great beauty, imposing yet delicate at the same time. In his 1821 novel *The Pirate*, Sir Walter Scott wrote of the palace that it has 'even in its ruins, the air of an elegant yet massive structure, uniting, as was usual in the residence of feudal princes, the character of a palace and a castle.'

The main front is the most striking, particularly the left-hand range. Whilst the ground floor ('below stairs') is quite plain, the upper floor ('the noble floor') is stylishly elaborate. Two tall, massive turrets project from the left, carried on rows of chequered corbelling. To their right are the corbelled bases of

Below: The Earl's Palace from the west, showing, on the first floor, the exterior of the Earl's private apartment and the great hall to its right.

two of the large oriels lighting Earl Patrick's great hall, one circular and one multi-angular. When complete, these windows must have been unsurpassed in Scotland. The corbelled breast of one of the great hall fireplaces completes the range.

The main entrance, in the angle between the two ranges, has an elaborate 'frontispiece'. Weathering has removed much of the detail in the three panels, but the lowest panel, in the quasi-classical lintel, bore an inscription, the middle one Earl Patrick's coat-of-arms, and the topmost panel those of James VI. The date 1607 is said to have been legible on the doorway at one time. Elsewhere, gun holes abound – saying much about the character of the man responsible for this architectural feast.

Above: The main entrance doorway to the Earl's Palace, with its elegant columns and frontispiece above.

THE GROUND FLOOR

The feeling one gets on entering the front door is that this palace is no run-of-the-mill Scottish laird's house. Another feeling one gets, though only after a good deal of inspection, is that the owner of this house was not just motivated by the needs of comfort and style but also by the requirement for privacy and security.

The entire ground floor is stone vaulted. Two corridors lead away from the entrance lobby, one running along the north range to the north-west tower, the other along the back of the south range to the kitchen. In the angle where the two corridors meet is the well. It seems awkwardly placed, but the use of alternating red and yellow sandstone in its construction (the same as in the cathedral) tells us that it was dug in the 12th century, to serve the original Bishop's Palace complex. The well recess, however, is entirely the work of Earl Patrick.

THE KITCHEN AND CELLARS

The spacious kitchen was intended to be smaller but was extended westward during construction; the construction joint can be seen running across the vault. The window (north side) and wall cupboard (south side) in front of the broad fireplace were probably intended to be inside the original unfinished fireplace, whose north side is visible. It is interesting that the kitchen fireplace has no oven; perhaps a bakehouse and brewhouse were provided in the ruined section further to the west. Elsewhere on the ground floor are cellars, six of them, each formerly holding different foodstuffs – barrels of meal and salted fish, carcasses of butcher meat and game – and drink – ale for the servants, fine wines for the earl and his guests.

Above: Looking out from one of the ground-floor gun holes. The Earl's Palace was besieged in 1614, during the rebellion of Earl Patrick's son Robert (see page 14).

Below: This hatch in the east wall of the kitchen acted like a 'dumb waiter', enabling communication with servants on the landing of the main stair.

Opposite: The corridor along the south range of the Earl's Palace, looking towards the 12th-century well.

THE UPPER FLOORS

The main stair leading to the first floor is a handsome scale-and-platt, with broad landings linked by straight flights of steps. The door leading off to the right at the top led into the main guest chamber, which was shut off from the rest of the palace and furnished with a couple of lockers and a latrine closet.

Across the head of the stair, on the right, is one of the most beautiful and intriguing rooms in Scotland. It served as an ante-room to the great hall, perhaps a waiting room where those seeking an audience with the earl would have awaited their summons. Opposite was the steward's room, for the official responsible for the smooth running of the palace. It has a fireplace, two-tiered locker and latrine closet.

Above: The ceiling of the ante-room, described as the 'little vaulted chamber' in an inventory of 1653.

One can visualise the earl's right-hand man peering out through the window overlooking the entrance court, keeping a note of those coming and going.

The great hall was one of the noblest state rooms of any private castle in Scotland. Even in its present roofless condition it impresses – well-proportioned, finely wrought and wonderfully lit by oriels to east and west and a great three-light window at the south end, beside the stair. The door to the right of the great hall's end-wall fireplace led into Earl Patrick's four-roomed private apartment. Two rooms occupied the rest of the first floor and two the floor above, linked by a spiral stair. Only the two first-floor rooms survive, the 'outer room' and the 'inner room'.

Above (left): The great hall's main fireplace, shown here, is a massive 5m (15 feet) wide. A coronet and the initials PEO (for Patrick, Earl of Orkney) are visible, though badly worn, on both columns.

Above: The great hall as it might have appeared in Earl Patrick's time, showing its fine painted ceiling.

EARL'S PALACE

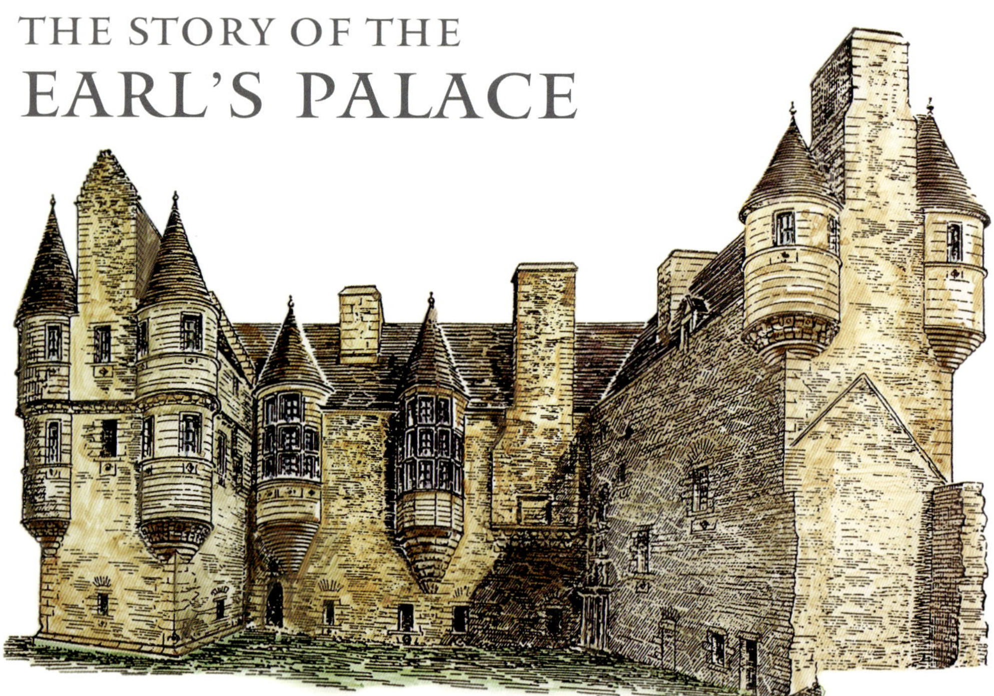

Above: The main front of the Earl's Palace as it might have appeared when complete.

Earl Robert Stewart, an illegitimate son of James V, acquired the episcopal lands and revenues of the Northern Isles in 1568 and ruled over them as Earl of Orkney until his death in 1593. His son, Patrick, succeeded as earl and it was he who built the Earl's Palace.

Father and son exercised unimaginable tyranny over their subjects. The sordid details do not concern us here, but the following extract from the record of Earl Patrick's trial in 1610 is significant for the information it gives about his architectural undertakings:

'The said Earl, leaving no sort of extraordinary oppression and treasonable violence unpractised against the inhabitants of Orkney and Shetland... has compelled the most part of the gentlemen tenants to work to him all manner of work and labour by sea and land, in rowing and sailing his ships and boats, working in the stone quarry winning and bearing forth stones... loading his boats and shallops with stone and lime, and loosing [unloading] the same, building his park dykes, and all other sorts of servile and painful labour, without either meat, drink or hire.'

In other words, Patrick built his castles with slave labour. In Kirkwall he built the Earl's Palace, and remodelled the Bishop's Palace to complement it. He also redesigned his father's palace at Birsay, installed a noble spiral staircase at Noltland Castle, on Westray, and in Shetland built himself a fine tower house at the ancient capital, Scalloway.

What astonishes us about Earl Patrick's castles is their extraordinary beauty and refinement, without parallel in Scotland – and this was a man whose execution had to be delayed whilst he was taught how to recite the Lord's Prayer! Their spacious and masterly planning and scholarly refinement reveal a man not only of large ideas but of cultured taste. All show the same high architectural distinction. In Tingwall churchyard, near Scalloway, is the tombstone of Andrew Crawford, Earl Patrick's 'maister of wark'; the name of the earl's master mason, John Ross, is known from record. These three men may well have combined to create this unique group of buildings – and the oppressed Orcadians and Shetlanders as well, of course!

Above: The tombstone of Andrew Crawford, the man who designed Earl Patrick's buildings, stands in Tingwall churchyard in Shetland.

SCALLOWAY CASTLE
Earl Patrick forces his subjects on Shetland to build Scalloway Castle.

PATRICK'S EXECUTION
Earl Patrick is executed in Edinburgh, not for his treatment of his subjects but for treason.

THE PALACE AFTER EARL PATRICK

After Earl Patrick's execution in 1615, the palace seems to have fallen into decay, 'ruinated by the weather'. However, two leading noblemen occupied it briefly in the mid-1600s. The first, in 1650, was James Graham, the first marquis of Montrose and leader of the Royalist forces against Scotland's Covenanting armies. In the 1640s Montrose recruited in Orkney for Charles I, before his defeat at Philiphaugh in 1645. He returned to Orkney in 1650 to recruit yet more

Above: The cathedral of St Magnus, with the walls of the Earl's Palace behind, from an early 19th-century painting by William Daniell. The level of the Peerie Sea, in front of the cathedral, is much higher than it is today.

troops, this time in support of Charles II, only to be defeated again and condemned to death by the Scottish Parliament.

The other aristocratic occupant of the Earl's Palace, in 1653, was Sir William Douglas, the ninth earl of Morton, who had an inventory drawn up of the accommodation. This document survives and makes very interesting reading. The rooms appear to be listed in the order in which they were visited, starting at the far end of the earl's apartment and working outwards, through the hall and guest chambers to the ground-floor service rooms: 'my lord's cabinet roume'; 'the bedchamber'; 'the roume ower the bedchamber'; 'the roume ower the dining roume'; 'the dining roume'; 'the great hall'; 'Bess Webb's chamber'; 'the doctor's chambers'; 'the utter roume entring from the hall'; 'the inner roume'; 'the two rounds'; 'the little vaulted chamber'; 'kitching' and 'bruehouse'.

Not until 1671 did the palace again become the bishop's residence, and so it remained until the last bishop, Murdoch Mackenzie, died there on 17 February 1688. With the final abolition of episcopacy in Scotland in the following year, the palace passed out of use and was left to fall into ruin. Both palaces were entrusted into state care in 1921.

Above: The Sheriff's Court, seen from the Earl's Palace. Since the Earl's Palace's abandonment the grand courtyard has gone, and so also the seamless link with the Bishop's Palace, rent asunder in the 19th century by the construction of the courthouse and Watergate.

1650

1689

MARQUIS OF MONTROSE

The marquis stayed in the Earl's Palace before mounting his last campaign against the Covenanters.

DECLINE AND FALL

With the abolition of episcopacy, the Earl's Palace falls out of use.

The Bishop's and Earl's Palaces, Kirkwall, are two of over 40 Historic Scotland sites on Orkney and Shetland, a selection of which is shown below.

Noltland Castle

↗ On the island of Westray, 1m W of Pierowall village.

🕐 Open all year

📞 01856 841815 (Skara Brae)

🚗 Approx 29 miles from the Bishop's and Earl's Palaces

Hackness Martello Tower and Battery

↗ At the SE end of Hoy

🕐 Open summer only

📞 01856 841815 (Skara Brae)

🚗 Approx 24 miles from the Bishop's and Earl's Palaces

Facilities

Earl's Palace, Birsay

↗ In Birsay on the A966

🕐 Open all year

📞 01856 721205 or 01856 841815 (Skara Brae)

🚗 Approx 18 miles from the Bishop's and Earl's Palaces

Scalloway Castle

↗ In Scalloway, 6m from Lerwick on the A970

🕐 Telephone Skara Brae (below) for opening times

📞 01856 841815 (Skara Brae)

🚗 Approx 150 miles from the Bishop's and Earl's Palaces

Facilities

For more information on all Historic Scotland sites, visit **www.historic-scotland.gov.uk**
To order a wide range of products and tickets, visit **www.historic-scotland.gov.uk/shop**

Key to facilities

Admission charge	£
Car parking	P
Interpretive display	
Picnic area	
Toilets	
Visitor centre	i